AF484542

Unfinished Conversations

The Words We Almost Said

Akshat

BookLeaf Publishing

India | USA | UK

Copyright © Akshat
All Rights Reserved.

This book has been self-published with all reasonable efforts taken to make the material error-free by the author. No part of this book shall be used, reproduced in any manner whatsoever without written permission from the author, except in the case of brief quotations embodied in critical articles and reviews.

The Author of this book is solely responsible and liable for its content including but not limited to the views, representations, descriptions, statements, information, opinions, and references ["Content"]. The Content of this book shall not constitute or be construed or deemed to reflect the opinion or expression of the Publisher or Editor. Neither the Publisher nor Editor endorse or approve the Content of this book or guarantee the reliability, accuracy, or completeness of the Content published herein and do not make any representations or warranties of any kind, express or implied, including but not limited to the implied warranties of merchantability, fitness for a particular purpose.

The Publisher and Editor shall not be liable whatsoever...

Made with ♥ on the BookLeaf Publishing Platform
www.bookleafpub.in
www.bookleafpub.com

Dedication

To the ones who never heard the words they deserved.
To the ones who held words too heavy to speak.
To the ones who needed to say goodbye, but never
could.
To the ones who found meaning in the silence.
This book is for you.

Preface

There are words we say, and then there are words we
never do.
Some fade before they reach our lips. Some stay trapped
in our hearts, waiting for the right moment—that never
comes.
This book is about those words.
The ones that almost became a conversation but didn't.
The ones that lingered in glances, in silences, in the
spaces between what was said and what was meant.
Through these poems, I hope you find pieces of your
own unfinished conversations. Maybe in a memory that
still stings, in a love that never fully bloomed, or in the
quiet strength of moving forward. Maybe you'll find
closure. Or maybe you'll just find comfort in knowing
that you're not alone in leaving things unsaid.
Some conversations remain unfinished, but that doesn't
mean they weren't worth having.

Acknowledgements

Every word in this book exists because of the people who shaped me—the ones who stayed, the ones who left, and the ones who lingered in between.
To my family, for their unwavering support and for understanding my silences just as much as my words.
To my friends, for listening to my unfinished thoughts and reminding me that not everything needs to be complete to be meaningful.
To the moments—both fleeting and lasting—that taught me the value of what remains unsaid.
And to you, the reader. If you've ever held words in your heart that never found their way out, I hope this book makes you feel seen. Thank you for letting these poems become a part of your story.

1. The first Goodbye

I was too young to understand what leaving meant,
too small to question why some doors close
and never open again.
But I remember the way the air felt different that day—
like something had been taken,
like silence had settled where your voice used to be.

No one told me that goodbyes don't always come with
warnings,
that sometimes they arrive unannounced,
a quiet thief in the middle of an ordinary afternoon.
One moment, you were here—laughing, existing,
and the next,
you were a space no one knew how to fill.

I searched for you in the corners of the house,
in echoes of old conversations,
in the way the walls still held your shadow.
I thought if I was quiet enough, still enough,
maybe I could hear your footsteps

one last time.

But goodbyes are never that kind.
They don't wait for you to be ready.
They don't pause to see if you can handle the weight.
They just happen, like the setting sun,
like the turning of a page you weren't done reading.

And maybe the hardest part of the first goodbye
isn't just losing someone—
it's realizing that loss doesn't come with instructions.
That the world doesn't stop,
even when your heart does.
That you still wake up the next morning,
still breathe, still move,
even when a part of you is stuck
in the moment they left.

And maybe, just maybe,
that's the cruelest truth of all—
that life moves on,
even when you're not ready to.

2. Paper Boats and Promises

We were young enough to believe
that paper boats could reach the ocean,
that wishes whispered into the wind
would always find their way back home.
With stained fingertips and careful folds,
we built our fleet—
delicate, weightless, invincible in our eyes.

We knelt by the water's edge,
bare feet sinking into soft mud,
watching our dreams set sail
on ripples that carried more than just paper—
they carried our belief in forever.
"One day, we'll follow them," you said.
"One day, we'll go wherever the waves take us."

But the wind turned restless,
the current pulled harder than we expected,
and one by one, they tipped—
our boats, our promises,

our childhood dreams.

We tried to save them, wading in too deep,
but paper isn't meant for storms,
and neither were we.

Years later, I stand by that same river,
watching the water take what it wants.
And I wonder—
was it the boats that weren't strong enough,
or was it us, believing they could last?

Maybe childhood isn't about dreams that survive,
but about the ones we dared to set free.
Maybe the promises that mattered
weren't the ones we kept,
but the ones we believed in long enough
to make them real.

3. The things They never said

They never said that love could be quiet,
that it could slip into the room
hidden in the scent of morning tea,
stitched into freshly folded clothes,
pressed into the softness of a forehead kiss
given too quickly to remember.

They never said *I'm proud of you*
in the way we saw in movies—
no grand speeches, no teary-eyed confessions,
just a silent nod when we did something right,
a heavier silence when we didn't.

They never said *I'm sorry*
for the nights we cried ourselves to sleep,
for the times their words cut deeper
than they ever intended,
for not knowing how to be gentle
in a world that never was to them.

They never said *It's okay to fall apart.*
Instead, they taught us how to hold things in,
how to carry our sadness like a well-packed suitcase,
how to smile even when our hands ached
from holding too much.

But maybe love was never in the things they said.
Maybe it was in the way they waited at the window
long after we were supposed to be home.
Maybe it was in the way they saved the ripest mango,
the softest roti, the biggest piece of anything—
always for us.

Maybe love was in the things they never said—
not because they didn't want to,
but because they didn't know how.

4. The Silence Between Us

Love lived in the quiet spaces—
in the pause between a question and its answer,
in the glance that lingered just a second too long,
in the way your hands hovered,
almost touching,
but never quite.

It was in the evenings spent side by side,
watching the sky shift from gold to dusk,
both waiting for the other to break the silence.
In half-smiles across crowded rooms,
in the soft sighs before parting ways.

In the way you always knew
how I take my tea,
though I never once told you.
Some loves are spoken into existence,
loud, certain, unafraid—
ours was etched in the spaces in between,
delicate as breath on a cold windowpane,

visible only to those who knew where to look.

But silence is a fragile thing,
and love unspoken is love unheard.
I wish I had known sooner
that even the loudest hearts
fade into echoes
if they never learn how to say,
"Stay."

5. A Letter to my Younger Self

Hey, you.

I know you're scared,
holding your dreams like fragile glass,
afraid the world will be too rough with them.
I wish I could tell you—
not everything will break.

You will outgrow the people
you thought would always stay,
and it will hurt.
But I promise,
some will stay longer than you expect,
and a few will come back when you least expect.

You'll lose yourself more than once,
but each time,
you'll find pieces you never knew were missing.
You will learn that happiness isn't a destination,

that love doesn't always mean forever,
and that failure is just another word for *try again.*

You'll make mistakes,
the kind that keep you up at night,
the kind that teach you things
no book ever could.
Forgive yourself anyway.
You won't always be strong,
but you will always be enough.

Even on the days when you don't believe it.
So hold on.
And when the world feels too heavy,
remember—
you make it lighter just by being here.

With love,
The You Who Made It.

6. The Almost-Love Story

We were everything but a beginning.
A half-written sentence,
a song that faded before the chorus,
a firework that never touched the sky.
We existed in late-night conversations,
in laughter that lingered too long,
in the spaces between friendship and something more.

But we never named it.
Maybe we were too scared,
maybe we already knew—
some stories aren't meant to be told in full.
I still remember the way you looked at me,
like you wanted to say something
but never did.

And maybe I should have asked,
but silence was easier
than risking the truth.
We were almost.

Almost something real,
almost something that could have stayed.

But love is not built on hesitation,
and we waited too long to be brave.
So now, we are just a memory—
a could-have-been,
a should-have-tried,
a love story
that never learned how to begin.

7. We Were Just Kids

We never saw it happening.
There was no final goodbye,
no dramatic ending,
just the slow unraveling of a thread
we didn't know we were holding.

We were just kids—
barefoot on burning pavement,
laughing until our stomachs hurt,
swearing we'd never change.
We spoke in inside jokes,
wrote our names in the dust on old school desks,
believed that forever was something we could hold.

But forever is fragile,
and life has a way of pulling people apart
without asking for permission.
One missed call,
one unanswered message,
and suddenly, the silence stretched too wide to cross.

I wonder if you ever think about it—
the summer afternoons,
the secrets whispered under borrowed blankets,
the friendship we thought was unshakable.
I wonder if, somewhere in another life,
we still find our way back to each other,
laughing like we did when we were just kids.

8. Unsent Texts, Unfinished Calls

I still have them saved—
half-written confessions,
words that never made it past my fingertips.
A hundred different ways to say *I miss you,*
but none that felt quite right.

"Hey, how have you been?"
Backspaced. Rewritten. Deleted again.
Because what if you've moved on,
what if my name no longer sounds familiar?

I almost called once.
Almost let the phone ring.
Almost let my silence turn into sound.
But what if you didn't pick up?
Worse—what if you did,
and I had nothing left to say?

So instead, I keep my words tucked away,

stored in the quiet corners of my heart,
with all the other things I meant to say.
Because maybe some goodbyes
are meant to stay unspoken,
and some messages
are never meant to be sent.

9. If I Had said 'Stay'

I wonder—
if I had said it,
if the words had broken past the fear,
if I had let my heart spill
before you walked away,
would it have made a difference?

Would you have turned around,
hesitated for just a second longer,
looked at me the way you used to—
like I was something worth staying for?

Or were you already half gone,
one foot out the door,
long before I found the courage
to reach for your hand?

Maybe love is not just about feeling,
but about speaking,
about saying the words

before they become ghosts
haunting empty rooms.

And maybe—
maybe if I had said *stay*,
I wouldn't be here now,
whispering it into the silence
where you used to be.

10. The Echo Of Your Name

You are not here,
but sometimes, it feels like you never left.

I hear your name in places we once belonged to,
in the hush of a song we loved,
in the way the wind moves through quiet streets.
It lingers in conversations
where I almost say your name,
but swallow it down like a secret.

Some people leave footprints
too deep for time to erase.
They exist in muscle memory—
in the way my hand still reaches for yours,
even when I know you're not beside me.

In the way I turn to share a thought,
only to remember
that you are no longer mine to tell.
But maybe leaving isn't the same as being gone.

Maybe we live forever
in the hearts that refuse to let us fade.

And maybe that's why,
no matter how much time passes,
your name still feels like home.

11. Conversations with a Ghost

I still talk to you.
Not out loud—
not in the way I used to,
but in the quiet moments
when the world forgets to be loud.

I tell you about my day,
about the things you would've laughed at,
about the people you would've loved.
I ask you questions
I know you'll never answer,
but somehow, I hear you anyway—
in the rustling leaves,
in the way the rain taps against my window,
in the hush of my own breath.

Grief is a strange thing.
People say we move on,
but I think we just learn

to carry ghosts gently.
To make space for them in our hearts,
to keep their voices alive
in the conversations
that no one else can hear.

So I'll keep talking,
because forgetting was never an option.
And maybe, just maybe,
somewhere beyond what I can see,
you're still listening.

12. A Room Full Of Empty Chairs

Once, this room was full.
Laughter bounced off the walls,
promises sat comfortably between us,
and the air was thick with the kind of certainty
that only youth and naivety can afford.

We swore we'd stay—
through distance, through change,
through the slow unraveling of time.
But forever is a fragile thing,
easily misplaced
between unanswered texts
and goodbyes that never felt like goodbyes
until the silence made them so.

Now, the chairs are empty,
their ghosts still lingering
in inside jokes no one remembers,
in stories that end with,

"You had to be there."

I still set places for the ones who left,
still catch myself waiting
for voices that no longer call this place home.
Maybe some people aren't meant
to stay till the last page.

Maybe their chapters end
long before we're ready to close the book.
But even now, in this quiet,
I like to think a part of them still lingers—
in echoes, in memories,
in the spaces they once filled.

13. The Last Thing You Said

I replay it like a song stuck in my head,
the last thing you said before the door closed,
before the call ended,
before I realized it was the last time.

Maybe it was something simple—
"Take care."
"See you soon."
Words that weren't meant to be final,
yet they turned into tombstones
I visit more often than I should.

Or maybe it was something heavier—
a truth I wasn't ready for,
a goodbye I didn't believe,
a promise that never had the chance to be kept.

The world moved on,
but I stayed there,
holding onto your words like a rope,

as if pulling hard enough
could bring me back to that moment,
to you.

But echoes don't answer back,
and last words don't change,
no matter how many times
I whisper them into the dark.

So I keep them close,
press them into my palms like prayers,
let them remind me
that once, even at the very end,
you still had something to say.

14. The Road Not Taken, The World Not Spoken

Regret is not a thunderclap.
It does not arrive in storms,
demanding to be seen,
heard, felt.

It lingers—
in the pauses between conversations,
in the almosts and the never-was,
in the sigh that escapes
before sleep takes over.

I think of the roads I didn't walk,
the doors I never knocked on,
the hands I should have held tighter,
the words that trembled at the edge of my lips
but never learned to fly.

"I should have told you."
"I should have stayed."

"I should have tried."

But regret is a silent thing.
It doesn't scream;
it just sits beside you,
an old friend who never leaves,
a shadow you carry
on roads you never meant to walk alone.

And maybe, if I listen closely,
it's not regret at all,
but the voice of the past
gently asking me to be braver next time.

15. Where Do Unfinished Stories Go?

Do they vanish—
like ink fading under the sun,
like pages left blank,
like voices that once filled the air
but now exist only in echoes?

Or do they stay,
woven into the spaces between our ribs,
stitched into the silence of 3 a.m.,
waiting for us to pick up the pen again?

Maybe they live in the songs
we can't listen to anymore,
in the letters we never sent,
in the places we once swore
we'd visit together.

Maybe they breathe in the pauses
between "Hello" and "How have you been?"—

in the way we hesitate,
wondering if reopening the book
will hurt more than leaving it closed.

Not every story finds an ending,
not every thread is tied,
but I like to think unfinished stories
don't just disappear.

They live on in us—
in the maybes, in the what-ifs,
in the quiet hope
that one day,
somewhere,
the next chapter will begin.

16. Hello, Again

I ran into someone familiar today—
caught him staring back at me
through a foggy mirror,
like a face you half-remember
from an old photograph.

He looked younger somehow,
lighter, like the weight on my shoulders
hadn't reached him yet.
His eyes still held the kind of fire
I thought I had put out.

"It's been a while," he said,
hands in his pockets,
a little amused,
a little disappointed.

And I wanted to ask—
"Did I turn out the way you hoped?"
But I wasn't sure I wanted the answer.

He just grinned,
like he already knew what I was thinking.

"You were never lost,"
he said, leaning closer,
"You just stopped looking for me."
And maybe he's right.

Maybe I buried him under deadlines
and late-night thoughts,
under all the things I thought
mattered more than remembering myself.

So I take a breath,
meet his gaze,
and say the only thing
that feels right—
"Hello, again."

17. Some Things Don't Need Words

You never said, *"I'm proud of you,"*
but you always stayed up late,
watching from the doorway
as I tried to figure life out.

You never said, *"I love you,"*
but you always remembered
to bring an extra jacket,
even when I said I wouldn't need it.

You never said, *"I'm here for you,"*
but when the world got too loud,
you sat beside me in silence,
letting the quiet do the talking.

Some loves aren't written in words,
but in the way they linger—
in folded blankets,
in shared earphones,

in glances that say *stay*
without ever needing to ask.

Because sometimes,
the loudest love
doesn't make a sound.

18. The Apology I Never Gave

I practiced it a hundred times—
in the shower, in the car,
in the quiet corners of my mind
where you still existed.

I wanted to say, *"I'm sorry."*
For the words I left unspoken,
for the ones I threw too carelessly,
for the days I didn't try harder,
for the nights you needed me and I wasn't there.

But time moved faster than regret,
and by the time I was ready,
you were already gone.
So I carried the apology,
folded it small,
tucked it between pages of old conversations,
hiding it in the spaces
where your name still echoes.

And maybe—just maybe—
some apologies don't need to be heard
to set us free.

Maybe letting go
is the only way
to finally say it.

19. Letters to the Future

Dear Tomorrow,

I don't know your name yet,
or the roads you'll take me down.
I don't know the faces that will stay,
or the ones that will blur into memory.

But I hope you are kind.
I hope the storms don't scare you as much.
I hope the weight on your shoulders feels lighter.
I hope you learn that some goodbyes
are just beginnings in disguise.

I hope you find love—not the kind
that completes you,
but the kind that reminds you
you were whole all along.

I hope you laugh at things
that once made you cry,

and that you look back
with pride at how far you've come.

And if you ever feel lost,
just remember—
I was here once too,
writing this,
believing in you.

With love,
A version of you who never stopped hoping.

20. And Yet, We Go On

The world doesn't stop for heartbreak.
The sun still rises,
even when we wish it wouldn't.
The clock keeps ticking,
pulling us forward,
one breath, one step, one day at a time.

We leave behind words
we should have said,
conversations that never found an ending,
people we thought would stay.
But life doesn't wait for closure.
It just moves—
relentless, unbothered,
dragging us along
until one day,
we wake up and realize
we aren't hurting quite the same anymore.

The echoes of what-ifs grow softer.

The spaces they left behind
start filling with new laughter,
new love,
new stories waiting to be told.

We don't forget.
We don't erase.
But we learn—
to carry the weight a little differently,
to walk forward even with the ache,
to keep living,
even when we thought we couldn't.
And somehow,
without realizing when it happened,
we go on.

21. The Words We Almost Said

It always comes back to this—
the words left hanging in the air,
the almost-confessions,
the half-written goodbyes.

I wonder if you ever think about them, too.
The nights we sat in silence,
both waiting for the other to speak.
The look in your eyes
that begged me to say something,
but I didn't.

Maybe if I had reached for your hand,
maybe if I had said *stay,*
maybe if I had let you hear
the words tangled in my throat—
would the story have ended the same?

But life is not built on *maybes.*

And time does not wait
for the ones too afraid to speak.
So we move forward,
carrying the weight of almosts,
rehearsing the words
we should have said,
whispering them into the quiet
long after they've lost their meaning.

And yet, somehow,
I hope they still find you.
I hope, in some small way,
you already knew.

www.ingramcontent.com/pod-product-compliance
Lightning Source LLC
Chambersburg PA
CBHW061725130726

47996CB00006B/2512